DESIGN
MUSEUM

FIFTY
SNEAKERS
THAT
CHANGED
THE
WORLD

**ALEX
NEWSON**

conran
OCTOPUS

FIFTY
SNEAKERS

INTRODUCTION

Sneakers are a thoroughly modern item of footwear. Barely more than 150 years old, they have gone from niche and functional to fashionable and omnipresent. With various types of sneaker now considered acceptable footwear in virtually any situation, the sports shoe is no longer just a highly technical piece of performance equipment – it has made the transition to the high street.

Science and technology have traditionally been the catalyst for innovation in sneaker design – whether it has been studies of human motion by photographic pioneers like Eadweard Muybridge, or such wonders as vulcanized rubber and polyurethane foam created by material scientists. However, driven by these new technologies, it has been the willingness of designers and manufacturers to tear up the old ways of working and go back to designing from first principles that has provided so much innovation.

While this model of technology and innovation as the principal driver of visual style is still relevant, the influence of fashion on the design of sports shoes is stronger than ever. Just as design has helped to shape the development of sneakers, sneakers have also influenced design, art and popular culture. And sneakers, perhaps more than any other product, reveal the tensions and creative connections between the worlds of sport, design and fashion.

It is hard to avoid the fact that the sportswear and sneaker market is feeling increasingly homogenized: the three big manufacturers – Nike, adidas and PUMA – account for a considerable proportion of the market, and indeed of this book. That is not to say, however, that these large companies do not develop interesting shoes – in fact, far from it. One of the principal reasons for their continued success is how much of their resources are pumped back into developing new technologies and fresh visual styles.

Usain Bolt prepares to run, and win, the 100m sprint at the 2008 Olympics in his customized Puma 'Complete Thesus' running spikes.

Page 2: Michael Jordan wearing his famous Nike 'Air Jordan 1' sneakers.

THE ORIGINAL PLIMSOLL c.1850

Plimsolls – or, depending on where you are from, daps, gutties, sannies or pumps – set the foundations for the modern sports shoe. The need for plimsolls grew out of the burgeoning Victorian leisure industry, as the newly installed train network enabled British holidaymakers to travel to the coast in large numbers. To cope with the demands of a beachside holiday a new type of shoe, referred to as a 'sand shoe', began to emerge. Holidaymakers started wearing simple cotton canvas shoes with soles made from leather or rope. However, these were not particularly resilient to water, and it was not long before the New Liverpool Rubber Company started to make cotton canvas shoes with a rubber sole. The discovery of vulcanization, by American engineer Charles Goodyear, allowed rubber to be made stronger and more flexible, and also to be attached permanently to other materials, such as fabric. Despite this, the junction between sole and upper shoe remained a weakness and the New Liverpool Rubber Company introduced a tight band of elastic around the outside of the shoe that clamped the two together.

Sand shoes acquired the nickname 'plimsolls' sometimes after 1876 when a white line, called the plimsoll line, was introduced to the hulls of ships indicating the maximum depth to which the vessel might be safely immersed without taking on water. Similarly, the band around the outside of sand shoes could be used as an indicator to the wearer that they could stand in water up to this line without getting their feet wet.

A swimmer on the beach in Deauville, France, wears plimsolls in the summer of 1913. After their introduction, this new type of shoe became quickly popular throughout Europe, Australia and the United States.

'CHAMPION'

By the start of the 20th century the US Rubber Company had produced over 30 different plimsolls, all sold under a range of different names and brands. While most of the plimsolls were fairly standard, some of the more innovative designs saw a stitched leather collar introduced around the top of the shoes to help reduce stretching and improve the shoe's lifespan. It was around this time that an enterprising young advertising agent started to refer to plimsolls as 'sneakers', due to the fact that you could easily sneak up on people wearing them as they made so little noise.

The US Rubber Company decided to capitalize on the name and consolidated all their ranges under one name which it marketed as sneakers. It initially tried to use the name Peds – from the Latin for 'foot' – but this was already trademarked, so the name Keds was eventually chosen instead, and in 1916 the first mass-produced sneaker was released.

Although most often worn by tennis and basketball players, the 'Champion' was conceived as a multi-purpose sports shoe. Soon after its launch Keds released a new range called 'Triumph', with a more fashion- and leisure-focused angle, as well as a range called 'Kedettes', aimed at the women's market. The shoes remain in production today.

'CHUCK TAYLOR ALL STARS'

1917
Converse

The Converse 'Chuck Taylor All Star', the world's first sneaker specifically designed for basketball, was first produced by the Converse Rubber Shoe Company in 1917. However, it was not until 1923 that Chuck Taylor became the brand's ambassador and his name and now-famous signature ankle patch were added to the shoe.

Charles Hollis Taylor was a basketball player in an era when the game was a rapidly growing, but still predominantly amateur, sport. As a sports enthusiast, Taylor wanted a job that was also related to basketball and accepted a job as a salesman with the Converse Rubber Company. Taylor became such a successful travelling salesman and basketball evangelist that he was soon asked to help redesign the 'All Star'. After sales continued to soar, Converse added the Chuck Taylor name to the marque and the sneaker that we all now recognize was born.

The 'All Star' remains largely identical to designs worn at the start of the 20th century. Because of this, other modern designs now provide far better support and performance and it is now seldom used as a performance sports shoe. The 'All Star' is a perfect example of how the success of a product, initially developed for function, can change the perception of its design, elevating it to a position of style and fashion. Regardless of whether it is worn as a fashion or sports shoes, the 'All Star' is one of the best-selling sneakers of all time and remains the archetype for all basketball shoes.

Early Converse magazine advert dating from 1948.

During the first few decades of the 20th century basketball was an emerging sport which was not supported by the vast market for equipment and accessories that we see today. Indeed the original prototype for the 'All Star' was intended to be used by football and netball players until it was redesigned by Chuck Taylor.

'GREEN FLASH'

The origins of the Dunlop 'Green Flash' can be traced back to 1888 when a Scottish veterinarian, John Boyd Dunlop, invented the first pneumatic tyre and quickly went about setting up a rubber company to produce this remarkable new product. The company rapidly diversified and began to make new rubber products, starting with car and aeroplane tyres, before moving on to garden hoses and sports equipment such as golf and tennis balls. By this point Dunlop Rubber was one of Britain's largest companies and, with manufacturing divisions in Europe, Japan, Australia and the US, was one of the world's first multinational corporations.

After making a successful range of rubber boots, Dunlop purchased the New Liverpool Rubber Company, primarily for its expertise in producing early plimsolls (see pages 8–9). In 1929 the Dunlop Sports division launched the 'Green Flash', a design specifically aimed at the tennis market. At the time the 'Green Flash' was far and away the best tennis shoe available and was worn by professional players like Fred Perry, who wore the shoes when he won his three Wimbledon titles in the 1930s. In 1939 Dunlop's Australian division, Dunlop Footwear, hoping to replicate the success of the 'Green Flash', developed its own specialist tennis shoe, the 'Volley', which went on to become an exceptionally successful and influential tennis shoe.

While the 'Green Flash' has now been superseded by modern tennis shoes with superior performance, the design's retro appeal and unique sense of Britishness have ensured that it remains popular.

A view of the production line at Dunlop's Liverpool factory in 1931. Dunlop's purchase of the New Liverpool Rubber company enabled it to combine the more than a hundred years of manufacturing expertise that the two companies had amassed.

'JACK PURCELL'

1935
Goodrich (now
Converse)

John Edward 'Jack' Purcell was a Canadian badminton player who became world champion in 1933 and remained unbeaten for more than a decade until he retired in 1945. This was at the start of the era when sports brands were starting to seek major sports stars to sponsor and work with – think Chuck Taylor or Fred Perry. Goodrich, another rubber and tyre specialist that turned its attention to shoes, asked Purcell to collaborate with the company on developing a new high-profile shoe design.

Although not dissimilar to the other plimsoll-style sneakers around at the time, Purcell's design featured a toecap with an unusually moulded double profile. This gave the design its signature look and led to the cap being described as 'Purcell's smile'. However, it was not just for show as it also provided the extra support (missing from other sneakers) that Purcell felt was needed for badminton. While not as high profile as some of its contemporaries, the 'Purcell' has a distinct appeal and has been worn by many famous faces including James Dean and Steve McQueen.

In the 1970s Converse acquired the rights to the Jack Purcell brand and continues to make the shoes to this day.

Since the Jack Purcell brand was taken over by Converse there have been numerous collaborations resulting in limited-edition takes on the classic design.

This 2011 example by Comme des Garçons features the standard 'Purcell' silhouette covered in the fashion label's unmistakable bug-eyed heart logo.

JESSIE OWENS'S RUNNING SPIKES

Adidas is one of the world's most respected sports brands, consistently designing sneakers that have influenced the entire sports industry. The roots of the adidas company can be traced back to 1920 when two brothers, Adi and Rudolf Dassler, founded a company and started making sports shoes in the cramped confines of their mother's washroom. The brothers quickly made a name for themselves by producing high-quality running spikes for elite athletes. Their first major success came in 1936 when American athlete Jessie Owens won four gold medals at the Berlin Olympics while wearing Dassler shoes. In addition to medals in the 100m, 200m, 100m relay and long jump, Owens's spectacular success was hailed as a defeat for Adolf Hitler whose ideals of 'Aryan supremacy' were thereby challenged.

In 1949 Adi Dassler acrimoniously split from his brother and set up his own company, adidas. The first design registered by adidas was a training and running shoe made of elk leather. As well as being one of the first designs to include an orthopaedic arch support, it was the first shoe to feature the now-famous three-stripe logo.

Interestingly, Rudolf Dassler established a rival business – PUMA. These two companies – founded by warring siblings with headquarters in the same small town in Bavaria, Germany – both grew to become two of the largest sportswear manufacturers in the world.

Jessie Owens's spectacular achievement at the Berlin Olympics has come to be seen as a pivotal moment in the history of track running. Versions of running spikes had been used to help with traction and grip on footwear for centuries, but the Dassler brothers were renowned for the quality of their versions.

'SAMBA'

1950
adidas

Every brand has a handful of classic designs with which it will for ever be associated. The 'Samba', one of adidas's most recognizable designs, has been in production for over 60 years and remains as popular today as it was when launched.

Although it has been redeveloped and redesigned countless times, the origins of the 'Samba' as a football training shoe are still evident. With traditional studded boots proving particularly problematic on frozen ground, the distinctive gum sole was developed to perform just as well on icy ground as it did on inside surfaces. This helped establish the shoe's reputation as a great all-year-round training shoe.

The rise of five-a-side football during the 1980s saw the popularity of the 'Samba' grow, and through its association with the sport it also became a popular choice for British fans in the football terraces. This helped make the adidas 'Samba' – along with brands such as Stone Island, Fruit of the Loom and Burberry – a firm favourite with those who identified with a subculture and fashion referred to as 'casual'. This was typified by the football hooligans of the 1970s and '80s who didn't wear club colours or jersey for fear of drawing the attention of the police but instead wore combinations of European designer labels and sportswear.

Football supporters decked out in their 'casuals' brands in 1985.

Until the late 1990s, when rival manufacturers such as Nike, Umbro and PUMA all released new designs, the adidas 'Samba' was one of the only sneakers aimed at the indoor football market.

'SUEDE CLASSIC'

Sometimes the public perception and awareness of a design slowly evolve over time; on other occasions there is a particular moment that crystallizes a product's appeal, and which will for ever be associated with that particular design. While PUMA 'Classics' have been available for over half a century and are one of the brand's more successful silhouettes, there is one single image that has come to define them.

On 16 October 1968 African–American athletes Tommie Smith and John Carlos finished first and third in the Olympic 200m finals in Mexico. When receiving their medals, the two performed a Black Power salute throughout the playing of the American national anthem. They shared a pair of black gloves and removed their shoes, revealing black socks representing black poverty.

When removing his suede PUMAs, Smith left them on the top of the podium in clear view. The resulting images, broadcast across the world, became one of the most powerful symbols for the Civil Rights and Black Power movements that were committed to reshaping American society.

Although Smith and Carlos were initially condemned for their stand, with the International Olympic Committee criticizing them for 'advertising their domestic political views', opinion is very different today. Smith and Carlos are widely praised for their bravery and for putting their principles and beliefs before any possible personal repercussions. In 2005 a 6m- (20ft-) high statue was unveiled at their former university depicting them in their now-iconic pose.

While this gesture is obviously more significant as a defining moment in sporting, and indeed social, history, the now-famous images have helped link the shoe, and the brand, to this iconic moment.

Athletes Tommy Smith and John Carlos on the Olympic podium in 1968.

PUMA 'Classics' are also often called PUMA 'Clydes' and PUMA 'States'. While there are some very minor differences between the designs, such as a slightly thinner sole and small variations on the formstrip that runs along the side of most PUMAs, the silhouettes and design of all three are almost identical.

'STAN SMITH'

Stan Smith is a former world number-one tennis player and winner of two Gland Slam titles. However, like Chuck Taylor, he is perhaps now better known for giving his name to a famous sneaker than for his sporting exploits.

The adidas 'Stan Smith', the brand's first leather tennis shoe, is famous for its simplicity and understated design. Usually seen in an entirely white colourway, its two defining features are the three rows of perforations down each side and the sketch of Stan Smith that adorns the tongue. The perforations – practical inclusions designed for ventilation – are also a subtle way of introducing adidas's famous three stripes that are otherwise missing from the design.

The 'Stan Smith' was originally marketed as the 'Haillet', a very successful and high-selling design named after French tennis player Robert Haillet. When Haillet retired, adidas decided that it wanted to find a new athlete to represent the design, and in 1971 Stan Smith was chosen to be, quite literally, the new face for the sneaker. Apparently, Smith was never particularly involved in the design of the sneaker. His most important contribution was to ask for something to be done to stop the tongue sliding about. This eventually led to the addition of a small tab on the tongue through which the laces could be threaded – an innovation that is now common on many sports and leisure sneakers.

The understated style of the 'Stan Smith' has ensured its longevity as a design and style classic.

'MEXICO 66'

1966
ASICS/Onitsuka Tiger

Japanese sports shoe manufacturer Onitsuka Tiger was founded in 1949 by Kihachiro Onitsuka. Onitsuka was a former military officer who passionately believed that sport not only reinforced physical health and self-esteem, but also taught young people to observe rules and instilled discipline and good manners.

Onitsuka Tiger's 'Mexico 66' design was produced to coincide with the 1968 Summer Olympics in Mexico. After it was announced that the Mexico Games would be the first to be televised in colour, all the manufacturers began working on plans to make their logos and insignias as visible as possible. Unveiled at the pre-Olympic qualifying trials in 1966, the design saw the first application of the classic tiger stripes. While developed to provide an eye-catching design, the stripes also acted as additional support and helped eliminate stretching of the upper parts of the shoe. The motif was so popular that it has been used ever since.

Onitsuka Tiger is now a subdivision of the global ASICS brand. While ASICS focuses on new technologies and innovations, the Onitsuka Tiger lines represent its classic designs and its unique Japanese heritage.

The 'Mexico 66' design is probably the brand's most recognized design, with the now-famous yellow-and-black colourway worn by Bruce Lee in the 1978 film *Game of Death* and, more recently, by Uma Thurman in *Kill Bill: Vol 1* and *2* (2003 and 2004)

CUSTOM '#44'

Having spent the beginning of his career working for large shoe manufacturers, Paul Van Doren grew frustrated at seeing the majority of profits go to distributors and retailers. Doren's response was to establish his own company, Vans, with a simple aim – to cut out the middlemen and sell shoes directly to customers.

After investing considerable time and money assembling the equipment needed for production, Doren and his three co-founders opened their first store selling a very limited range of designs. Simply called '#44', the first design was based on a classic rubber-soled deck shoe but developed to be better quality and harder-wearing than their competitors' shoes. To achieve this, they used the strongest canvas they could source and made the soles almost twice as thick as anything else available.

The small capacity of the initial factory had some obvious advantages and disadvantages. They were unable to make enough stock to provide a wide range of styles, or choices in colour or fabric. However, this was countered by the fact that, because manufacturing was small-scale, it could be easily changed and adapted. As they controlled the production of the shoes in a nearby factory, Vans began to offer a custom service, making the '#44' out of scraps of fabric brought in by customers. This trend quickly caught on with the local community, and customers started to have shoes made from things like old school uniforms and cheerleading outfits.

Initially, Vans '#44' was available only in four colourways – navy blue, white, green and red. However the instant success of the custom service saw people use increasingly unusual and creative fabrics and prints.

'SUPERSTAR'

Originally released as a basketball shoe, the adidas 'Superstar' was nicknamed the 'shell shoe' owing to its recognizable rubber-shell toe piece. However, the design eventually gained popularity not as a sports shoe, but as a fashion icon of one of the late 20th century's most significant music and cultural phenomena. During the late 1980s the popularity of the 'Superstars' reached new levels when adidas embarked on a ground-breaking collaboration with Run-DMC. Run-DMC represented a new breed of hip-hop artists who, instead of dressing in the slightly flashy style of previous generations, developed a more natural street style typified by tracksuits, Kangol hats and unlaced sneakers.

The unlaced sneakers were a fashion statement said to originate from prisons where inmates were not allowed to have shoelaces in case they hanged themselves. Run-DMC were so fond of adidas 'Superstars' that in 1886, partly as a response to an anti-sneaker rap song by Gerald Deas called 'Felon Sneakers', they released the single 'My adidas'. Quick to spot an opportunity, adidas offered Run-DMC a sponsorship deal worth over $1.5 million. This ground-breaking collaboration was the first time that a sports manufacturer had gone to such lengths to forge such a strong connection with music, particularly given the fact that hip-hop was a still a small and commercially unexploited subculture.

Almost overnight, Run-DMC, supported by their collaboration with adidas, had helped take hip-hop music and fashion from a marginalized underground scene to a mainstream style. In 2002, when one of Run-DMC's founding members, Jam-Master Jay, was shot and killed, fans and friends and mourners left piles of adidas 'Superstars' outside his New York recording studio as a mark of respect.

Run-DMC seen wearing the adidas 'Superstars' they were so fond of.

The rubber-shell toe piece meant that the 'Superstar' became commonly known as the 'shell toe'.

'CORTEZ'

1972
Nike
Bill Bowerman

Nike is without question the largest and most influential manufacturer of sportswear in the world. However, compared with companies such as Converse, Reebok and adidas, it is still a relatively new brand. The history of Nike can be traced back to the late 1950s when Bill Bowerman, the track and field coach for the University of Oregon, worked with a student athlete named Phil Knight. In 1964 the two established the Blue Ribbon Sports Company to import and distribute shoes made by Onitsuka Tiger (see pages 26–7). However, after a few years Bowerman began experimenting with his own sneaker designs. Starting out as revamps of Onitsuka designs, his work developed and eventually led to what would become Nike's first commercially available shoe, the 'Cortez'. With Bowerman continuing to look after the design and Knight managing the business side, the two founded Nike to produce and sell the shoe.

As much of the design work on the 'Cortez' was carried out when Bowerman was working with Onitsuka Tiger, the Japanese manufacturer also released a design with the same name. This was virtually identical to the Nike version apart from featuring the tiger logo instead of the Nike swoosh. However, Onitsuka soon changed the name of its sneaker to the 'Corsair', which has since become a classic in its own right.

The jogging craze that hit the US in the 1970s and Nike's pivotal role in it were referenced in the 1994 film *Forrest Gump*, in which the central character played by Tom Hanks wore a pair of 'Cortez' in the classic red-and-white colourway during all the jogging scenes.

The 'Cortez' was the shoe that launched Nike. The release, in 1972, perfectly coincided with the US jogging boom and the company rapidly expanded to meet the rising demand.

'THE WAFFLE TRAINER'

1974
Nike
Bill Bowerman

Bill Bowerman, Nike's co-founder and first chief designer, was known for experimenting with ideas, processes and unusual ways to innovate. One of the more extreme stories dates from his time as the athletics coach at the University of Oregon when the university replaced their athletics track with a new artificial surface. Traditional running spikes were no longer suitable and Bowerman began to investigate how he could create a sole that better gripped this new running track.

The solution to the problem was found in the most unlikely of places. According to Bowerman's wife, the two were eating waffles one morning when Bowerman turned the waffle upside down and suggested that the lumps and ridges of the waffle might be the perfect shape to grip the new running track. To test this idea, Bowerman quickly fetched the necessary materials and poured liquid polyurethane into the family waffle iron.

The resulting design was further refined, and in 1974 it was incorporated into a design sold by Nike known as the 'Waffle Trainer'. Owing to the unusual pattern of the sole, the resulting footprints were similar to those left by astronauts, causing the shoes also to be referred to as 'Moon Shoes'.

Bowerman's hands-on approach to tinkering and prototyping – all done with the aim of giving his athletes, and then later his customers, a performance advantage – resulted in him being inducted into the American National Inventor Hall of Fame.

Bill Bowerman's unconventional use of a waffle iron has become part of footwear design folklore. However, his unusual approach was just another example of his continual pursuit of production and material innovation.

During the 1970s the general public, especially in the United States, became increasingly concerned with health and fitness. This fitness craze saw an explosion of interest in activities like jogging and aerobics. It also opened up enormous and profitable new markets to sportswear companies. As the amount of money coming into the industry grew, so did the money spent on research and development. This led to a rise in the technical development in sportswear not seen since the invention of photography had first allowed shoe designers to study the biomechanics of the foot.

US manufacturer New Balance was at the forefront of this new jogging craze and was one of the first companies to use scientific methods to test and evaluate shoe designs. After consulting podiatrists, physiotherapists and doctors, it developed a far more comprehensive understanding of what happens when we run and how the resulting shock from each step is transferred through the foot and up into the body.

Researchers found that, broadly speaking, there are three different styles of running: *neutral*, where the foot travels in a straight line as it moves forwards; *pronation*, where the foot rolls inwardly from the heel; and *supination*, where the foot rolls outwardly from the heel. As well as offering shoes in a variety of width fittings, New Balance was the first manufacturer to offer running shoes that specifically catered to these differing styles.

New Balance's commitment to comfort has been evident since the company was founded in 1906. Originally called the New Balance Arch Support Company, it specialized in manufacturing insoles and arch supports rather than shoes. It produced its first pair of shoes, a pair of kangaroo-leather running spikes, in 1938.

'BATA x WILSON x JOHN WOODEN'

1977
Bata

The idea of a joint venture between Bata, one of the world's oldest and most venerable shoe companies, and John Wooden, one of the United States' best-known and most respected basketball coaches, seemed like a great fit. Here was the opportunity to develop a new basketball shoe that could forsake gimmicks and showy marketing tricks in pursuit of a design that would be genuinely focused on performance and progressive thinking.

Rather than having a sole made from vulcanized rubber, as was the case for virtually every other basketball shoe, the 'Bata x Wilson x John Wooden' used polyurethane, a compound almost entirely new to shoe manufacturing. Polyurethane consists of tiny air bubbles packed together to provide an effective combination of absorption and durability. Another advantage is that different densities of the compound can be achieved by varying the quantity of bubbles. This changes the weight of the material and also enables a shoe sole to be created that provides different degrees of absorption in different areas depending on where it is needed.

Unfortunately, the design was in production only for a year and is now extremely rare. While the shoe is relatively unknown outside of the world of sneaker enthusiasts, its impact was enormous and polyurethane soles are still used today in a wide range of different shoes.

Perhaps most commonly used for more active footwear, such as sports shoes and hiking or trekking boots, polyurethane's exceptional durability has led to it being commonly used in the production of soles for business and leisure shoes as well as safety footwear.

'AIR TAILWIND'

1978
Nike

Following the explosion of interest in jogging during the 1970s, a period of intensive development and innovation saw the introduction of an array of new sneaker technologies. Among the many solutions were designs with gel and foam inserts and soles, as well as more dramatic solutions such as the Reebok Pump. Nike's response to this technology arms race, the Air system, stands head and shoulders above the others. Decades later, Nike Air technology is still influencing footwear design and continues to be used in the production of high-performance sports shoes.

The Air system was developed in 1977 by the aerospace engineer Marion Frank Rudy who was working for Nike as an independent contractor. Technically, the initial system was not actually air but consisted of a pressurized gas housed in a thin polyurethane casing.

Nike quickly incorporated the technology into a running shoe and released the 'Tailwind' just in time for the 1978 Honolulu Marathon. Although runners were initially sceptical and worried that the air pocket might burst mid-race, anyone who tried the new design was an immediate convert and the first batch of shoes quickly sold out. There were even stories of the people invited to test crude, half-finished prototypes having refused to return them.

This extraordinary success compelled Nike to introduce the technology into other disciplines including basketball ('Air Force 1', 1982) and tennis ('Air Trainer 1', 1987). Although updated to account for modern materials, the Air system is one of Nike's key technologies and is still used across most of its brands.

In 2012 Nike celebrated the 'Tailwind' by introducing a model that was closely modelled on the innovative 1978 original.

All the sportswear and sneaker manufacturers were quick to cash in on the jogging craze that swept across the United States in the 1970s.

ADICOLOR SERIES

The idea of customizing our shoes is an old one. Brands often develop new styles and trends by observing how individuals and subcultures use and customize their sneakers. This can be seen with brands like adidas, which quickly learned from the merger between hip-hop and sportswear (see pages 30–1), as well as brands like Vans, which started producing designs specially designed for skateboarders after seeing how the skating community was using and hacking their trainers (see pages 62–3).

In 1983 adidas took this notion one stage further and created a range of shoes that encouraged and actively facilitated self-customization. The Adicolor series provided classic adidas silhouettes that were sold in pure all-white versions along with specially developed waterproof and quick-drying pens for people to showcase their individuality and unique designs. In 2006 the idea was further developed with new Adicolor ranges based on specific colour themes, this time including acrylic paints and spray cans as well as pens.

While a combination of advances in modern manufacturing and sophisticated website interfaces now allows us to virtually customize our shoes before they are made, the original Adicolor pre-dated all of these developments. As well an innovating on existing customization trends, the Adicolor project was also a harbinger of what was to come.

The 2006 Adicolor series included a pack of six spray cans with which customers could customize the all-white sneaker. An accompanying marketing campaign was produced to appear as if the posters and billboards had been graffitied with spray paint.

'AIR JORDAN 1'

Nike
Peter Moore

Even in an industry that has embraced celebrity endorsement and sponsorship deals like no other, there is one deal that stands head and shoulders above the rest. In 1984 a young Michael Jordan signed a deal that not only helped Nike become the world's pre-eminent sports brand, but also changed the way sneakers are marketed. Michael Jordan had never before worn Nikes, previously preferring to wear Converse or adidas, but was convinced to sign after being presented with sketches of what his new shoe would look like, a video highlights package of his best moments (set to the soundtrack of the Pointer Sisters' hit song 'Jump') and half a million dollars.

The first 'Air Jordan' might not have had the technology seen in later models, but the combination of a winning young athlete and a great-looking shoe, designed in black and red to match the colour of Jordan's team, the Chicago Bulls, captured the public imagination. The famous 'Jumpman' logo was taken from a silhouette of Jordan performing his trademark dunk. First used in 1988, it was developed to work perfectly alongside the brand and has been ever-present since.

The Air Jordan range has been continually expanded and developed, with, to date, more than 20 iterations of the sneaker and countless other spin-off products. In 2013 alone, ten years after he retired, Jordan still received almost $100 million from Nike in sponsorship and royalties. Not content with designing one of the most influential sneakers of all time, Peter Moore left Nike to become Creative Director at adidas where he developed the three stripes logo that the company still use today.

The original red-and-black colourway was actually banned by the authorities as it did not contain enough white. However, Jordan wore it anyway, receiving a paltry fine every match, a fact that was spun by Nike's marketing team, who positioned the 'Air Jordan' as the choice of rebellious youth.

PEG SYSTEM

1984
adidas

After the launch of the Nike Air system (see pages 40–1), other sports shoe brands launched competing cushioning technologies. While ASICS were developing its gel system and Reebok was planning the Pump (see page 54–5), adidas was first to market with its new big initiative – the peg system. Shoes incorporating the peg system had three holes bored through the side of the midsole that were filled with a series of different-coloured pegs. The colour coding of these pegs was important as it corresponded to different densities. Users could use a specially designed tool to swap these pegs around and customize the degree of support and cushioning as they required.

The peg system was included in a series of adidas shoes including the 'Grand Slam', the 'Kegler Super' and the 'L.A. Trainer'. The system was also used by German tennis player Steffi Graf, who was often seen using the peg system in 1988, when she won all four of the tennis Grand Slams as well as a gold medal at the Seoul Olympics.

Just like the Nike Air system, especially as deployed in the 'Air Max' (see page 52–3), the peg system provided a clear visual indicator of the technology. The manipulation of such overt visual language can be vital in the successful promotion of new technologies. It can act as a type of logo for the technology, signposting its presence to potential new consumers each time a pair of shoes is worn.

Steffi Graf in action at the 1988 US Open wearing adidas 'Grand Slams', which included the customizable three-peg system.

The peg system, or 'Vario Shock system' as adidas calls it, was included in the 'L.A. Trainer' launched in 1984 to coincide with the Los Angeles Olympic Games.

GUCCI TENNIS

1984
Gucci

There was almost nothing about Gucci's design that made it stand out from the hundred other tennis shoes of the era. It had no new technology or material innovations, nor at first glance did it look unique – instead aping the style of classic tennis shoes from the late 1970s. However, what it did have was a Gucci logo emblazoned on the tongue, a stamp promising 100 per cent hand-stitched genuine Italian leather and a price tag so ludicrous that it began a trend that would influence the sports industry and luxury brands for decades to come.

We are familiar with seeing the trickle-down effect of high-end fashion on the high street. However, the Gucci shoe demonstrated the trend working in reverse, and showed that the world of sport was now capable of influencing the world of luxury brands. This two-way trading of ideas and inspiration is commonplace today. Maison Martin Margiela produces shoes that reference German Army trainers; Rick Owens has mimicked the 'Air Jordan'; and Karl Lagerfeld has launched New Balance–inspired designs. However, it was the 'Gucci Tennis' shoes that were the first example of a luxury fashion house turning to the world of sport for inspiration. Essentially a status symbol, it was also the inspiration behind Jay Z's 'Carter S' design for Reebok in 2003.

The 'Gucci Tennis' shoe was not really meant for playing tennis in. It was all about the combination of a classic tennis-shoe silhouette and US hip-hop street culture, with the added kudos of a luxury European fashion label.

'AIR TRAINER 1'

1987
Nike
Tinker Hatfield

The *enfant terrible* of tennis, John McEnroe was a controversial and sometimes abrasive character. Known for his temper and on-court tantrums, he was also very charismatic. Nike first approached McEnroe with a prototype version of a new shoe design with a thick Velcro strap placed over the laces rather than in the conventional location around the ankle. Although McEnroe was given clear instructions that the shoes were still in development and not to be worn in public, he was filmed competing in them a week later at an international tournament. After being confronted by Nike, he reportedly told them that they had nothing to worry about as the shoes were 'the best tennis shoes you assholes ever made'. The prototype design eventually became the 'Air Trainer 1' and was officially endorsed by McEnroe for many years. Designed by Tinker Hatfield, the shoe was the first of a new breed of sneaker intended for multi-sport use.

Nike's first sponsorship deal was signed in 1973 when the Romanian tennis star Ilie Nastase began using and endorsing its products. Since then, this network of sponsored athletes has grown quickly, to the point where Nike now has the largest sponsorship budget of any sports manufacturer. While its long and productive relationship with Michael Jordan is often considered to be sport's most successful sponsorship deal (see pages 44–5), there have been many others that helped nurture the public perception of what a Nike athlete should be.

John McEnroe could not have been more different from Michael Jordan, but his association with Nike proved vital at a time when Nike was still establishing its brand.

The Nike 'Air Trainer 1' is regarded by many sneaker enthusiasts as the best ever sneaker design. Their argument is strong: not only was it hugely influential in terms of performance, paving the way for all the cross-trainer sneakers that followed, but stylistically it went on to affect many later designs, not least the 'Yeezy' (see pages 88–9).

'AIR MAX 1'

1987
Nike
Tinker Hatfield

Although the Nike Air technology had been around for almost a decade, it wasn't until the launch of the 'Air Max' that the silhouette we now associate with the Nike Air brand was created. With one relatively simple design feature – the insertion of a window in the sole revealing the air bubble – the 'Air Max' moved beyond the world of sport and into the street.

First hired by Nike as an architect, the 'Air Max' designer, Tinker Hatfield, quickly changed disciplines, bringing elements of the architectural process to the field of sneaker design. 'Air Max 1' – or 'Air Max '87', as it is often now called – is said to have been inspired by a holiday to Paris, when Hatfield visited the Pompidou Centre. Designed by architects Renzo Piano and Richard Rogers, the Pompidou Centre (completed 1977) is a ground-breaking building that moved all the usually internal elements of the building – the staircases, elevators, ventilation systems, ducting and so on – to the outside of the building. Emboldened by this dramatic building, Hatfield wondered how he could apply a similar aesthetic to shoe design. The idea of exposing the previously unseen was not the only idea Hatfield took from the Pompidou Centre. The bright-red colourway of the original design was supposedly inspired by the complex's brightly coloured façade.

Tinker Hatfield has been one of the world's most prolific and influential shoes designers, and over the past 30 years he has been responsible for some of Nike's most celebrated designs. Now Nike's Vice President for Design and Special Projects, Hatfield heads the 'Innovation Kitchen' in Oregon where most of the company's design and research take place.

According to Tinker Hatfield, Nike's marketing team was initially very reticent about the 'Air Max' design, worried how a sneaker whose major feature was a huge hole in its sole would be received by customers.

PUMP

Reebok
Paul Litchfield

While sometimes considered a poor cousin to Nike and adidas, Reebok has been responsible for some significant developments in the history of the sports shoe. During the 1990s it was the world's second largest sportswear manufacturer. It was the first brand to promote specifically to the women's sport market as well as being the first to realize the power of collaborating with a film star. However, one of Rebook's best-known innovations is the Reebok Pump.

The original concept behind the Pump was first developed by Reebok's in-house designer, Paul Litchfield, and the design and innovation consultants Continuum. Considered by some to be nothing more than a marketing gimmick, it enabled wearers to inflate the air-cushioned soles by squeezing a small pump, usually prominently located on the tongue. Introduced soon after Nike's 'Air Max', the Pump was actually a much more sophisticated system. The combination of pump and small release valve gave the wearer control over the degree of cushioning and support they wanted.

Now part of the adidas group and with headquarters located in the United States, it is easy to think of Reebok as just another large international sports brand, defined by its sponsorship deals with celebrities and high-profile athletes all over the world. However, originally founded in 1895 in north-west England, the company still retains a large part of its British identity.

Initially launched as a relatively casual mid-market running shoe, the Reebok 'Classic' gained a strong following with the UK youth market during the 1990s and 2000s and was seen as a British equivalent to the adidas 'Superstar'. Its popularity was helped by British pop stars such as Dizzee Rascal, Mike Skinner (aka The Streets), Pete Doherty and the Arctic Monkeys, all of whom have worn and sung about Reebok 'Classics'.

While the first design to use the Pump was a basketball high-top, Reebok used the same system for a range of styles – including a collaboration with US tennis player Michael Chang that featured an imitation felt-covered tennis ball as the Pump.

SHIMANO PEDALLING DYNAMICS (SPD)

1990
Shimano

Usually referred to as the SPD system, or even as SPuDs, Shimano Pedalling Dynamics is a type of clipless bicycle pedal that allowed cyclists to fasten their shoes into place on their pedals using specially designed locking mechanisms and corresponding shoe cleats. Clipless pedals, sometimes called clip-in or step-in pedals, are not a particularly new invention. The oldest examples date back to an 1895 design by a US inventor named Charles Hanson. However, Shimano's system was the first to really catch on and be used by professional and amateur cyclists.

The chief benefit of clipless pedals, aside from stopping feet from slipping off pedals on rough terrain, is that they maintain power on the upward stroke of each cycle revolution, helping to more efficiently transform the rider's energy into forward movement. One of the drawbacks with clipless pedals is that they are usually designed around a proprietorial system that needs specific cleats and pedals to work. However, as the popularity of SPDs increased, other manufacturers started to make shoes that worked with SPD pedals and the system became more universal. Companies like Quoc Pham, DZR and Chrome now specialize in making dual-use sneaker-style shoes that have built-in cleats for clipless pedals but can also be worn all day as a conventional pair of shoes.

Cycling shoes specialist DZR produces a wide collection of styles to suit individual tastes and cycling disciplines, including the 'Terra' sneaker designed for mountain biking. DZR also sponsors professional cyclists from a variety of disciplines, including downhill and cross-country mountain biking, urban cycling and even bicycle polo.

NIKE ANTI-SWEATSHOP CAMPAIGN

This is not a story about the impact of a particular shoe but about a pivotal moment in the history of sneakers and how they are made. As sports shoes and sneakers started to become big business, most of the major manufacturers moved production to factories in Vietnam, China, South Korea and Taiwan, where cheap labour was plentiful and less regulated. During the 1990s reports began to surface about the terrible conditions inside these factories. This included accusations of child labour, unsafe practices, abusive management and pitiful wages.

During the 1990s there was a consumer-led campaign to boycott Nike products. The campaign included mass demonstrations, negative publicity, mainstream media coverage and boycotts. This eventually led to Nike installing a code of conduct in its factories and increasing transparency around activities and conditions.

Although the campaign focused on Nike, largely owing to the size and profile of the company, it was far from alone in having the ethics of its manufacturing called into question. Similar stories were surfacing about many other Western manufacturers that were producing goods in the Far East. This included other sports brands as well as clothes shops, supermarkets and electronics stores. While the situation is considerably better than before, there remains unease in some quarters that an industry that delivers affordable products to the Western world is so dependent on the exploitation of workers in developing countries.

In 2001 the American Internet entrepreneur Jonah Peretti reopened the debate when he tried to have the word 'sweatshop' embroidered on a pair of sneakers using Nike's new online customization service. While Nike declined to make the shoes, the series of emails between Nike and Peretti was published on the Internet.

During the many protests that took place Nike was often the target of demonstrators' anger, with placards, banners and posters brandishing variations on Nike's famous slogan 'Just Do It' proving particularly popular.

DISC SYSTEM

PUMA has a history of innovating sports shoe fastening mechanisms. In 1968 it became the first manufacturer to use Velcro, an innovation that was soon picked up by others and is now commonplace in sports shoe design. Although it may not have proved so influential, PUMA's other big fastening innovation, the Disc system, was perhaps even more radical.

The original Disc system features a series of lightweight wires running around the shoe that can be tightened by turning a circular disc that sits on top of the tongue. The chief benefit of the Disc system is that the wires can be integrated much further into the structure of the shoe, rather than just tightening the shoe at the top where the laces are located, and thus providing a much tighter fit. The disc can also be infinitely and easily adjusted without having to retie the laces simply by giving the disc a turn one way or the other. However, while there were undeniable benefits to the technology, there were also some significant drawbacks, not least the additional weight of the disc and the related system of integrated wires.

Although the Disc system never had the impact that PUMA would have liked, it is a feature to which it returns from time to time in its contemporary designs, although usually in casual and fashion sneakers rather than in sports ranges.

PUMA rightly claimed that the Disc system provided a closer fit and therefore a performance advantage. This was backed up by their initial marketing slogans such as 'Turn it on' and 'Win. Lose. Never tie.'

'HALF-CAB'

1991
Vans
Steve Caballero

While Vans started out by making simple but well-built deck shoes (see pages 28–9), during the 1970s it began to gain a reputation within California's growing skateboarding scene. The extreme durability of the shoes' design coupled with the anti-slip nature of the high-quality rubber sole ensured that they were perfectly suited to the rigours of skateboarding.

Vans cultivated this new following and started to produce shoes specifically designed for skateboarders. Vans's famous checkerboard design was launched in the 1980s when Steven Van Doren, the son of the brand's founder, Paul, noticed a group of skateboarders drawing on their shoes with felt-tip pens.

In 1989 Vans partnered with skating superstar Steve Caballero, who gave his name to a new sneaker aimed at skaters who were using purpose-built ramps and skate parks. The hi-top design was perfect for this type of 'vert-ramp' skating as it provided additional support and protection around the ankle. However, during the early 1990s skating styles started to change and the scene became dominated by street skating – a style that used narrower skateboards with smaller wheels, making tricks more manageable.

Caballero noticed that skaters were regularly cutting down the ankle support and taping it in place. After trying the trick himself Caballero found it perfect for this new style of skating and took the idea to Vans, which put this new silhouette into production. Known as the 'half-cab', it has gone on to become one of Vans's most popular designs.

Skating shoes hacked down and gaffer-taped in place provided skater Steve Caballero with the inspiration for the half-cab, as shown here in an edition celebrating 20 years since the shoe's release. Caballero was known for his difficult tricks and technical style and is credited with popularizing vertical ramp skating.

'PREDATOR'

1994
adidas
Craig Johnston

Craig Johnston is a South African–born Australian footballer who, after retiring from professional sport, felt that he could do a better job of creating the football boots that he used to play in. Rather than simply improve on the existing design, Johnston wanted to develop a new type of football boot, one that would allow footballers to play the game in a way that was not possible during his career. Johnson used rubber to build up a series of ridges and grooves around the toe and top, instead of using the leather that made up the rest of the boot. These ridges were intended to give players more control over the football, and theoretically even affect the flight of the ball after it was kicked.

After initially being rejected by adidas, Nike and Reebok, Johnston enlisted the help of two former international German footballers, Franz Beckenbauer and Karl-Heinz Rummenigge, who in a short promotional film demonstrated the boots in snowy conditions. Subsequently convinced of the design's potential, adidas purchased the rights and developed it further.

There was widespread interest in the 'Predator' boot when it was released as a commercial product, with the new technology being worn by a number of elite footballers including Zinedine Zidane and David Beckham.

The 'Predator' boot became popular with footballers who specialized in free kicks, corners and long-range strikes. Celtic's John Collins became the first professional footballer to score a goal wearing 'Predator' boots when he scored from a free kick on the edge of the penalty box against local rivals, Glasgow Rangers, in April 1994.

'PELOTA'

Even though the Camper name was established only in 1975, the history of the brand can be traced back through four generations of a family shoemaking business founded in Mallorca, Spain. Camper refers to its different shoe silhouettes as belonging to 'families' grouped together by 'concepts'.

First produced in 1995, the concept behind the 'Pelota' was inspired by the passion and imagination of the pioneers of sport – and especially by the traditional designs of early American sports shoes used in baseball and basketball. Camper shoes have always been distinctive. And it is no surprise that its range of sneakers looks unlike any others on the market.

The most recognizable and indeed unusual feature is the sole, which is comprised of 87 individual balls made from natural rubber. These different-sized rubber balls are placed in carefully designed arrangements where they can provide the perfect balance between absorption, comfort and grip. This unusual feature, although functional in its inspiration, has created a powerful and individual visual style that has since been copied by many other manufacturers.

The word *pelota* – Spanish for 'ball' – relates to the 87 balls featured on the sole. The 'Pelota' is one of the oldest silhouettes in the Camper range and remains one of the most popular designs they sell.

PLATFORM SNEAKERS

Buffalo

Initially reintroduced by fashion designer Vivienne Westwood, the early 1990s saw extreme platform shoes make a return to fashion. In 1993 the trend captured the public imagination when supermodel Naomi Campbell took a high-profile dive on the catwalk while wearing a pair of super-elevated platform shoes during a Westwood show.

Unsurprisingly, it was not long before the trend filtered down to the high street. One of the more unusual developments was a new hybrid style that crossed platform shoes with sneakers. The trend was best captured by another 1990s phenomenon, the Spice Girls, whose high-platform sneakers were an important part of some of the group members' carefully constructed personas. Although many manufacturers jumped on the platform sneaker bandwagon – including budget retailers such as Tesco – it was the German brand Buffalo that kicked off the trend and provided the Spice Girls with their signature footwear.

Clothing and accessories brand Buffalo Boots was founded in 1979 predominantly as a retailer of cowboy boots, which at the time were particularly popular with the youth market. As youth trends changed, so did Buffalo, and by the 1990s it had established a sports shoe line. Continuing to respond to trends in the youth markets, Buffalo developed a range of platform sneakers that proved highly popular – albeit only for a short time. As well as being favoured by the Spice Girls, Buffalo platforms were worn by other celebrities including Cher and Madonna.

Spice Girl Emma Bunton wearing platform sneakers in 1997.

'AIR FOAMPOSITE 1'

1997
Nike
Eric Avar

Most famous sneakers gain their reputation through a combination of new technologies and unusual or original visual styles. More often than not, it is the performance innovation and the technology behind it that lead to the new aesthetic. Inspired by a beetle's carapace and a sunglasses case made from hard plastic foam, the Foamposite range is the perfect illustration of this principle.

While the majority of sports shoes still used stitched-together leather or canvas, the upper element of Foamposites was made from a single piece of moulded polyurethane foam. It required a manufacturing process so unlike anything previously used in the shoe industry that, until Korean car company Daewoo helped develop a workable manufacturing solution, there were genuine concerns that it was unrealizable. Foamposites are made by boiling the polyurethane material until it can be poured into a specially created mould before it cools and solidifies.

For all the talk of manufacturing innovations, the most important aspect is the eventual performance. As well as being considerably more durable, the design provided a glove-like fit that actually conformed to the foot as it was worn, resulting in exceptional cushioning and comfort.

All this innovation came at a cost and the high retail price initially hampered sales of the shoe. However, the technology has now been incorporated into many of Nike's other ranges and new Foamposite designs are now among the brand's most sought-after sneakers. Now Nike's Vice President of Innovation, designer Eric Avar has worked for the company since 1991 and been responsible for some of their most forward-thinking designs. Concentrating predominantly on basketball Avar has worked on the Hyperdunk and Kobe lines as well as the Foamposite range.

The Nike Air Foamposite 'Galaxy' was released in 2012 and created especially for the NBA All star game. Along with the Foamposite design, Nike also released a series of other sneakers that featured similar motifs and graphics inspired by NASA and space travel.

The Nike Air Foamposite 'Pro Volt' was an all-neon-yellow version launched in 2014.

MASS CUSTOMIZATION

1999 —
Nike, Vans, etc.

Until relatively recently the only way to own a bespoke shoe was to pay a specialist shoemaker to hand-make a one-off design. This exceptionally expensive solution ensured that customized shoes were a luxury available only to the very wealthy. Bar a few exceptions, such as Vans Customs, most people were restricted to selecting a design from the wide selection of mass-produced shoes available.

However, recent years have seen advances in manufacturing, especially digital manufacturing, that make it possible to mass-produce unique and individual products. This disrupts the traditional manufacturing model based around economies of scale, ultimately meaning that it is not always necessary to make hundreds of thousands of identical copies of a product in order to make it affordable.

As well as developments in manufacturing, there have also been advances in websites, software and systems that help facilitate mass-customization. Consumers can now use simple online applications to customize their shoes before they make a purchase, empowering them to create something unique and personal. It is now possible to select a style of shoe, choose the colour of individual elements and select from a palette of different materials and finishes. It is even possible to have text embroidered on the side of the shoes.

Nike was the first brand to provide an online customizable service, with the launch of NIKEiD in 1999. The other brands were not far behind, however, and we now have similar services offered by PUMA, adidas, Converse, Vans and countless other manufacturers.

Screenshots showing the customization interface on the Vans website. While most of the large sportswear brands now offer a customization service, the interface and degree of customization available can be very different. Some brands offer detailed colour and material choices that affect all elements of a shoe, while other, simpler systems restrict customers to a handful of choices usually regarding just colour.

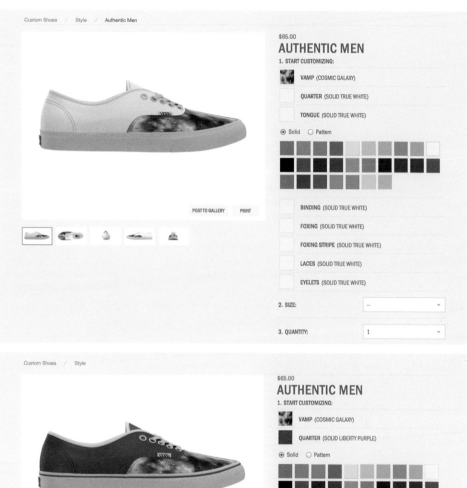

$65.00
AUTHENTIC MEN
1. START CUSTOMIZING:

VAMP (COSMIC GALAXY)

QUARTER (SOLID TRUE WHITE)

TONGUE (SOLID TRUE WHITE)

⦿ Solid   ○ Pattern

BINDING (SOLID TRUE WHITE)

FOXING (SOLID TRUE WHITE)

FOXING STRIPE (SOLID TRUE WHITE)

LACES (SOLID TRUE WHITE)

EYELETS (SOLID TRUE WHITE)

2. SIZE: --

3. QUANTITY: 1

POST TO GALLERY   PRINT

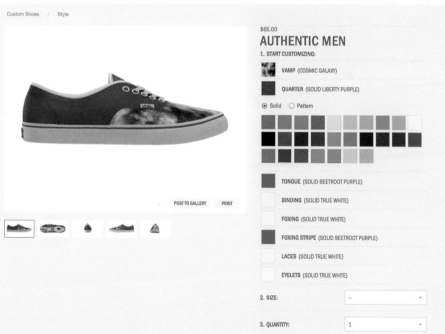

$65.00
AUTHENTIC MEN
1. START CUSTOMIZING:

VAMP (COSMIC GALAXY)

QUARTER (SOLID LIBERTY PURPLE)

⦿ Solid   ○ Pattern

TONGUE (SOLID BEETROOT PURPLE)

BINDING (SOLID TRUE WHITE)

FOXING (SOLID TRUE WHITE)

FOXING STRIPE (SOLID BEETROOT PURPLE)

LACES (SOLID TRUE WHITE)

EYELETS (SOLID TRUE WHITE)

2. SIZE: --

3. QUANTITY: 1

POST TO GALLERY   PRINT

'AIR WOVEN RAINBOW x HTM'

2002
Nike
HTM

There have been a handful of sneakers using Nike woven technology, but the limited-edition Rainbow range was the most eye-catching. The shoes were woven from stretch nylon that was dip-dyed in various colours to ensure that no two pairs were the same. Although the original woven shoes were quite difficult to produce, requiring various complicated and sometimes handcrafted processes, their impact has been enormous. They are very much the forerunners of a technology that has been incrementally refined, before culminating in the digital knitting technology that underpins the Nike 'Flyknit' (see pages 98–9).

HTM is a design collective or supergroup that represents three of the most creative and renowned sports shoes designers working today – Hiroshi Fujiwara (musician and designer), Tinker Hatfield (Nike's Vice President for Design and Special Projects) and Mark Parker (Nike's CEO) – whose collaborative work has led to some of the most innovative sports shoe designs in recent years. Although HTM usually designs sneakers with a new and inventive visual twist, it is always the new technologies at the core of the design that drive the visual language and innovation. This is why HTM is often the first to explore new technologies developed by Nike before they are rolled out and incorporated into existing shoe designs.

The 'Air Woven Rainbow' was something of a departure for Nike, which previously had rarely released shoes aimed at the leisure market. It was also a testing ground for the HTM collaboration, whose projects – in the words of Nike CEO Mike Parker – were intended to 'amplify new innovations, reinterpret existing designs, and explore concepts that take the brand to new places'.

NIKE LASER PROJECT

2003
Nike
Mark Smith

Nike's so-called Innovation Kitchen is where the majority of the company's new technologies are envisaged and developed. As an essential part of the company's continuous growth, it provides the link between its core business and the ideas that drive future business. Developed from inside the Innovation Kitchen, the Laser Project is a perfect example of how Nike uses innovation to drive growth.

Using lasers is nothing particularly new in manufacturing; they have been used for decades to cut precision components based on instructions translated from computer files and designs. The process is very similar to how a desktop printer works, except that the printer head that jets out ink has been swapped for a laser. Nike was already familiar with using lasers to cut custom parts from leather and other materials, which would then be sewn or glued together to create prototype shoes. In 2003, however, Nike designer Mark Smith wondered how this technology could be used to provide decoration and embellishments instead of just aiding the construction.

Smith experimented by cutting series of complex geometries and patterns in the shoes' panels as well as etching shapes and illustrations into their surface by reducing the intensity of the laser. Nike decided to take this process to production and commissioned a series of illustrators to work on limited-edition designs that would be laser-etched on to the shoes' surface, creating intricate marks on the leather like a tattoo on skin.

One of the primary advantages of using a computer-controlled laser to decorate a shoe is the level of accuracy and intricacy that can be achieved. As the machine is capable of creating patterns accurate to a fraction of a millimetre, the details in some of the designs can only be fully appreciated at close range.

'AIR FORCE II x ESPO'

2004
Nike
ESPO (Stephen Powers)

During the 1990s Stephen Powers was an active member of the United States' underground graffiti movement, working under the name ESPO ('Exterior Surface Painting Outreach') and well known for large conceptual pieces in and around New York City and Philadelphia. Powers has since moved from the graffiti world to working as a professional visual artist, combining exhibiting at prestigious international art shows such at the Venice Biennale, with undertaking large-scale public commissions like his 'A Love Letter for You' project, for which he painted a series of more than 50 murals along an elevated train route in Philadelphia.

For his collaboration with Nike, Powers chose to work with one of his favourite classic designs, the 'Air Force II'. Although there are some obvious references to Powers's visual style, such as the big graphic text banners wrapped around the heel, the shoe's most obvious design feature was the replacement of the upper and side panel of the shoe with a clear material. As an accompaniment to the unusual see-through windows, the shoes were sold with a pair of specially designed socks. While this design was one of the more extreme limited editions produced by Nike, it proved very influential and inspired a mass of copies and fakes over the following years.

Stephen Powers's reworking of the Nike 'Air Force II' was part of the company's second iteration of its 'Artist' series, which also featured designs by Pharrell Williams and, rather confusingly, Halle Berry. While the other two designs have now been consigned to history, Powers's design has been well remembered and has proved remarkably influential.

'FIVEFINGERS'

2005
Vibram

In 1935, after witnessing the death of six companions during a mountaineering expedition in the Italian Alps, Vibram's founder, Vitale Bramani, vowed to develop footwear with better grip to ensure that nothing similar would ever happen again. After many years of producing high-quality footwear for mountaineering and climbing, Vibram used its experience of producing rubber soles with exceptional grip to branch out into other areas of shoe design.

Described as a foot glove or a second skin, the 'FiveFingers' was originally intended to provide sailors with good grip and the flexibility needed when moving about on the deck of a boat. However, as the design tightly conforms to the shape of the foot and accurately replicates the sensation of being barefoot, it has also become popular with 'natural runners'. Natural running – running with either no shoes or extremely lightweight and thin-soled shoes – has increased in popularity over recent years and companies like Vibram have been keen to capitalize.

In 2012 the company was sued over its claims that the 'FiveFingers' increased training efficiency and foot strength and decreased the likelihood of running-related injuries. While there is some evidence to support this, medical and scientific opinion remains very much divided, and Vibram has been forced to refrain from claiming any health benefits arising from wearing 'FiveFingers' shoes.

Most of the large sportswear manufacturers now produce shoes targeted at the natural running market. However, Vibram's 'FiveFingers' is among the only models with separate toe pockets: this slightly disturbing-looking innovation provides far greater individual articulation of the toes.

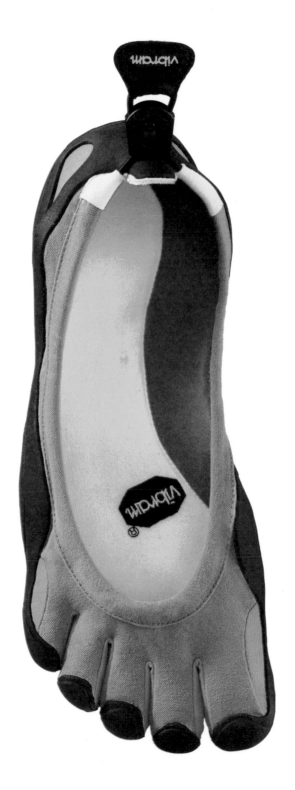

CUSTOMIZED 'COMPLETE THESEUS'

2008
PUMA

Usain Bolt is one of the most celebrated athletes of modern times. Although most people expected Bolt to win the 100m at the 2008 Olympic Games, the manner in which he achieved that victory was remarkable. By the time he crossed the line, in a new world-record time, he was so far ahead of his competitors that he had slowed to a virtual jog. As part of an arrangement with his sponsor, PUMA, Bolt ran in a pair of customized gold running spikes. After winning the race he removed the eye-catching shoes embroidered with 'Beijing 100m Gold' and held them up in front of the world's TV cameras.

Measuring the value and impact of a sponsorship deal is notoriously difficult. However, experts have estimated that Bolt's performances at the Beijing Olympics earned PUMA something in the region of £200 million in publicity. Although the amount PUMA paid Bolt to wear its brand and carry out various media duties has not been publicized, it surely represents good value and an excellent return on PUMA's investment.

The relationship between global brands and international sports stars is, of course, a professional one, with both parties usually gaining from deals. However, that does not preclude them from being meaningful and, on occasion, career-long partnerships. Rather than choosing to sponsor established stars, many brands actually look towards young talents in the hope that they will later become successful. This was the case with Bolt, whose relationship with PUMA began long before he was a world-record holder, when he was just a promising 17-year-old junior athlete.

Jamaica's Usain Bolt celebrates after winning the men's 100m final at the 2008 Beijing Olympic Games. Four days earlier, Bolt broke the men's 200m world record.

'JEREMY SCOTT x ADIDAS'

2008
adidas
Jeremy Scott

You do not have to look hard to find spectacular and exuberant sneaker collaborations. One of the principal reasons for commissioning limited-edition collaborations is to raise the profile of a brand by creating something unusual and unconventional. However, even in a market of ever-increasing hype, US fashion designer Jeremy Scott's designs for adidas stand out as something extraordinary.

Scott's first design for adidas was for a catwalk show in 2002 when he decorated a sneaker with a motif of American money that replaced the representations of George Washington with sketches of himself. Since the success of this design, adidas and Jeremy Scott have not looked back, moving from one collection to the next, with each delivering a more extreme and exaggerated design than the last. Many of Scott's designs use enlarged cartoon motifs to attract attention, whether this is a pair of wings, an enormously oversized tongue, a furry tail or a teddy bear's head. The sneakers might not be subtle but they are produced by a designer with a clear vision and a deft touch.

Since his debut collection in Paris in 1997 Scott has developed a reputation as an innovative designer who skilfully manipulates pop and youth culture references. This has helped generate success with younger audiences and led to his designs being favoured by celebrities such as Bjork and Nicki Minaj.

In 2013 Jeremy Scott continued his successful Adidas Original series with the 'JS Wings 2.0'. The design draws on the oversized wing motif previously used by Scott but rendered here in retro 8-bit black-and-white pixels.

'NIKE DUNK x LIBERTY'

2008
Nike

Some of the best collaborations are the ones that might not make much sense on paper but which, once realized, make you believe that the participants have been paired together for ever. Nike's collaboration with Liberty, one of Britain's oldest department stores, does exactly that. The contrasting styles of the two brands have seemingly little in common, yet the quintessential Britishness and period styling of Liberty's prints work remarkably well alongside the modern athletic silhouettes of the sneakers.

Liberty is particularly well known for its traditional prints, often characterized by gentle colour palettes and floral or paisley patterns. However, the store has also worked with modern designers to develop a contemporary range that complements these more traditional styles.

At the start of the Nike–Liberty collaboration in 2008, Nike was given full access to Liberty's archive of 43,000 prints. The shoe chosen for the initial collaboration was a 'Nike Dunk' – a bold choice given its large high-top style. However, the design was an immediate success, almost instantly selling out, leading to a series of further collections drawing on more and more of Nike's and Liberty's classic designs.

The success of Nike's initial collaboration with Liberty has led to a series of other capsule collections. This design from 2012 marries a classic paisley Liberty print with a Nike 'Hyperclave'.

'AIR YEEZY'

2009
Nike
Kanye West/Mark Smith

Taking its name from one of Kanye West's many nicknames, the 'Air Yeezy' is the fruit of a collaboration between Nike and the influential US rapper. This was an important and unusual departure for Nike, which, unlike most other brands, generally restricts its high-profile collaborations to athletes. The majority of celebrity collaborations are actually quite limited in their creativity, and often involve little more than the celebrity being sent an Illustrator file of the shoe for them to throw colours and patterns at.

Given the fact that we can all do this now via online customization, it is no surprise that this traditional concept of 'collaboration' has begun to feel dated. Rather than redesign a classic shoe silhouette, the development of the 'Yeezy' was more complex, with West and Nike's creative director, Mark Smith, working closely on an entire design.

The collaboration has so far produced two designs, the 'Air Yeezy', in 2009, and an updated 'Air Yeezy 2', in 2012. Borrowing a number of design features as well as manufacturing processes and tooling components from some classic Nike designs, the 'Yeezys' are as exuberant as you would expect. The hi-top-style sneakers feature many over-the-top design details such as an oversized Velcro strap and a ridged rubber heel. Both versions, sold in limited editions and in only a handful of colourways, immediately sold out and have since become among the most sought-after shoes on the market.

Kanye West has been frequently seen wearing his Yeezy designs, including during his performace at the 2009 G.O.O.D. Music Showcase in Austin, Texas.

A design sketch for the 'Air Yeezy 2'.

'CLEVER LITTLE BAG'

2010
PUMA
Yves Béhar

PUMA, more than most manufacturers, has been remarkably progressive about how it analyses the environmental impact of its business. In 2010 it established the first ever 'Environmental Profit and Loss Account', which assesses the environmental impact of a product at each stage of its life cycle. This includes the procurement and generation of raw materials, the production processes, and all the retail and consumer phases.

One of the first products to be assessed for environmental impact was not a sneaker but an associated product universal to all sneakers – the shoe box. PUMA asked Yves Béhar and his San Francisco–based design consultancy, Fuseproject, to see what improvements could be made to the whole distribution system. Over a period of two years Fuseproject looked at the way products are packed, the way they are shipped and stored, what consumers do with shoes boxes and the various recycling possibilities. The project's ultimate goals were to minimize the overall environmental impact and, where possible, to reduce costs.

The eventual solution was not to use a box at all but instead to use a bag with a minimal cardboard insert and heat-bonded seams. On the manufacturing side alone, the 'Clever Little Bag' has reduced water, energy and diesel consumption by more than 60 per cent. This equates to approximately 8,500t (9,370 s.t.) less paper consumed, 20 million MJ of electricity saved, 1 million litres (0.26 million US gal) less fuel and the same amount of water conserved each year. During distribution 500,000 litres (0.13 million US gal) of diesel are saved and, by no longer requiring us to use plastic bags to put the shoe boxes in, almost 275t (303 s.t.) of plastic are saved as well.

Yves Béhar and Fuseproject, the studio he founded in 1999, work on multidisciplinary projects that combine elements of business innovation, strategy, brand, digital, product and communications. Although Béhar has built up an extremely diverse portfolio of products, there are common threads that can be seen throughout his work – namely, sustainability and a sense of social purpose.

'ROLLER-BOAT'

2010
Christian Louboutin

Christian Louboutin shoes are not for the faint-hearted. Quoted as saying that he is not interested in comfort and that many of his shoes are not designed for walking in, Louboutin's approach to shoe design might not feel particularly well suited to sneakers. However, this slightly misses the point of what Louboutin shoes are about. The flamboyant, extreme, fantastical and occasionally fetishistic designs are not meant for everyday use, but are instead intended to be used more like costume pieces. Regardless of his indifference to his customers' comfort, Louboutin has developed a handful of casual sneakers, including a range of sneakers based on the classic plimsoll silhouette called the 'Roller-Boat'.

While Louboutin's sneakers are more accessible and less excessive than the majority of his shoes, they still carry a number of the stylistic devices that have become his signature – the most obvious being the metal studs that decorate and cover most of his sneakers. A handful of his sneakers also feature the glossy red soles that adorn the bulk of his womenswear designs. The red soles, often seen as emblematic for all Louboutin designs, are said to have come about when Louboutin, disappointed in a lacklustre shoe design, grabbed his assistant's red nail varnish to enhance it.

Louboutin sneakers may not be a high-street bestseller; indeed, they come with a price tag that certainly puts them out of reach of most casual sneaker fans. However, the lure of the Louboutin name and the popularity of the sneaker designs with celebrities like Elton John, Rhianna and Kanye West have resulted in cheap copies popping up everywhere.

Louboutin's 'Roller-Boat' sneaker is available in various colourways and styles. The inspiration behind the shoe was a desire to produce a more casual version of the designer's famous 'Roller-Boy' loafer.

'AIR MAG'

2011 (1989)
Nike
Tinker Hatfield

In 1989 when the makers of *Back to the Future: Part II* needed a futuristic sneaker for Michael J Fox's 'Marty McFly' to wear, they approached Nike to talk about having a new design especially made. Unsurprisingly, Nike leapt at the opportunity and gave the project to its head designer, Tinker Hatfield. The brief was a dream for someone like Hatfield who, unencumbered by technological and financial realities, was able to really let his imagination run wild and envisage the sneaker of the future.

In addition to its illuminated outer sole, the key feature of the 'Air Mag' was a self-lacing mechanism. These laces were shown automatically tightening as soon as a foot was inserted into the shoe. Along with other technological curiosities featured in the *Back to the Future* films, including a time-travelling DeLorean car and the hovering skateboard, Hatfield's futuristic hi-top sneaker really struck a chord.

While the design heavily influenced Hatfield's later work, especially the 'Hyperdunk' and the 2008 limited-edition 'McFly Hyperdunk', it was not until an online petition asking Nike to put the 'Air Mag' into production that the design became a reality.

In 2011 a limited quantity of 1,500 pairs were made and sold via auction, with the proceeds donated to the Michael J Fox Foundation for Parkinson's research. While the design looked like a genuine reproduction of the trainers previously seen only on screen, it was missing the all-important self-lacing technology. However, as Nike has already gained a patent for an automatically lacing trainer system, this may not be far behind.

Michael J Fox sitting on the bonnet of the DeLorean car wearing the 'Nike Mag'. In January 2015 Nike designer Tinker Hatfield claimed that his team was hard at work developing a working version of the self-lacing 'power lace' system.

MISSONI x CONVERSE
ARCHIVE PROJECT

2012
Converse
Missoni

Converse's First String line represents the brand's premium range. Sometimes a First String range focuses on a re-engineered and modernized design of an old silhouette, but usually these top-tier products will be limited-edition capsule collections developed in collaboration with an outside partner. Previous one-off collaborators have included Maison Martin Margiela, Bodega and Comme des Garçons, as well as regular partnerships with Italian fashion house Missoni.

Launched during Paris Fashion Week in 2012, the Missoni x Converse Archive Project revisited 20 discontinued fabrics from Missoni's extensive archive. Carefully chosen to represent a full range of Missoni designs, the selection included fabrics that debuted in catwalk collections from the early 1990s to some more contemporary designs. By selecting some more unusual choices from Missoni's heritage collection, the final choice of fabrics provided an accurate representation of the Missoni brand, and without succumbing to easy clichés such as only using the classic zigzag designs for which the brand is so well known.

The collection was limited to using just a handful of silhouettes from the Converse range. This included two lesser-known designs, the 'Auckland Racer' – a running shoe whose design dates back to pioneers of the jogging movement in the 1970s – and a basketball shoe – the 'Pro Leather Mid'.

This particular Missoni collaboration uses Converse's classic All Star silhouette (see pages 12–13).

'FLYKNIT RACER'

2012
Nike

Using an innovative digital knitting process, the entire upper element of the 'Flyknit Racer' is made in a single piece. This works in a similar way to how different patterns and structures can be incorporated into a knitted garment simply by changing the order and type of stitches. The 'Flyknit Racer' is produced in the same way, with the knitting pattern carefully designed to vary the structure of the knitted piece, and to provide different physical characteristics within a single piece of fabric. A close inspection of the shoes reveals how the patterns of intricately woven thread change dramatically – with denser patterns around the areas that require strength and support, such as the toes and ankle, and thinner, more transparent areas where air circulation and flexibility are required.

Although the complex engineering process took four years to develop, elements of its design can be traced back even further to technologies such as the 'Flywire' (2008) and Nike's first woven designs (2002; see pages 74–5). As the shoe does not contain multiple components, and has no need for joins, seams, stitches and so on, it can be designed to be stronger, lighter and more flexible, and results in less waste. Nike claims that the knitted upper is 20 per cent lighter than its average shoe and can reduce waste by up to 80 per cent.

As the knitted uppers are digitally produced, the ultimate aim of the technology is for a customer to be able to go into a shop to have their foot 3D-scanned and then have a shoe made that conforms precisely to their feet. While the 'Flyknit Racer' was developed as a running shoe, the range has been expanded: Flyknit technology is now being used to create high-performance designs for sprinting, basketball and football.

When using traditional manufacturing methods it is not unusual for more than a hundred people to have touched a pair of shoes during the production process. Nike's digital knitting technology dramatically reduces this number by automating a large part of the process.

'URBAN SWIFT'

2012
PUMA
Hussein Chalayan

In 2008 PUMA appointed Hussein Chalayan, twice winner of the British Fashion Designer of the Year award, as its creative director. Further demonstrating the increasing integration between the worlds of sport and fashion, the deal also included PUMA taking a stake in the Chalayan label.

Known for his architectural, technological and cutting-edge fashion collections, Chalayan makes catwalk garments that incorporate Arduino electronics, smart sensors, lasers and LED lighting. Alluding to the nature of speed in sport, Chalayan has explored the dynamics of kites and sails to transform his approach to tailoring. Other elements of the collections are inspired by Japanese kabuki theatre and dance. In keeping with Chalayan's previous work, his PUMA Urban Mobility ranges are collaborative projects that explore the undefined boundaries between fashion and technology.

While the collection includes both clothes and accessories, the 'Urban Swift' shoe was one of the key pieces. The shoe's unusual silhouette takes its inspiration from a series of rubber dresses developed for Chalayan's Spring/Summer 2009 collection 'Inertia'. Like the dresses, the rear of the shoe dissolves into a series of spikes achieved by injection-moulding thermoplastic polyurethane.

Most sneakers, especially those developed with performance in mind, have a visual sensibility that is born out of utility – they look as they do because of how they perform. As with Jeremy Scott's Originals series for adidas (see pages 84–5), PUMA has given Chalayan licence to go beyond utility. This does not mean that the resulting designs do not make use of high-tech materials and techniques, or do not respond to the demands of sportswear, but that they are not limited by traditional constraints.

Hussein Chalayan's designs for PUMA take sneakers beyond the confines of mere utility.

OSSUR FLEX-RUN WITH NIKE SOLE

2012
Ossur/Nike

Designed specifically for distance running, variations of the Flex-Run prosthetic limb have been used for over 20 years. These prosthetics help amputees of all abilities to achieve their athletic goals, whether that is a jog in the park, a triathlon or a world record. A recent version, developed in collaboration with Nike and American record-breaking Paralympian Sarah Reinertsen, has been redesigned to feature an interchangeable running sole.

The Nike clip-on sole features consolidated layers of thermal cushioning and air pockets that wrap snugly around the carbon-fibre running blade. Plastic tabs serve as fastenings that secure the sole in place and allow it to be changed quickly and easily.

Previously, athletes used to go through the laborious process of cutting away a sole from a standard pair of running shoes before attaching it to the bottom of the prosthetic. This was an inelegant solution to the problem, which lacked flexibility and was prone to failure at critical moments.

These J-shaped carbon-fibre prosthetics to which the Nike sole attaches are similar to Flex-Foot 'Cheetah' blades used by infamous South African Paralympian Oscar Pistorius. Described as passive-elastic springs, they are designed to emulate biological legs. They store and return elastic energy, but cannot generate net positive power or absorb negative power. The carefully calculated curve tapers into thinner carbon layering around the toes to provide added flexibility. The design of the original Flex-Foot 'Cheetah', first launched in 1996, was so well resolved that very little has changed since.

In many ways carbon fibre is a wonder material. It can be produced to be exceptionally, strong, while remaining flexible and lightweight. However, one of the qualities not usually associated with carbon fibre is grip. Nike's collaboration with Ossur solves this problem by providing a detachable sole that can be customized for various running surfaces and disciplines.

'CONCEPT 2'

New innovative equipment is vital to the development of sport. It helps keep it fresh and relevant and always moving forward. However, the boundaries between innovation and fair play can become blurred. What is sometimes referred to as 'technological doping' can prevent a sport from being a fair contest based on the individual merits of the athletes. The 'Concept 2' basketball shoe is a product that sits right on this line between innovation and unfair advantage.

Implanted in the sole of the shoe, under the balls of the feet, is an intricate spring-based propulsion system. Eight coil springs per shoe, held in place with specially designed plates, store energy from downwards pressure, which is released on take-off to increase lift.

After tests showed that this new technology can help athletes gain up to 9cm (3.5in) on a vertical jump, the National Basketball Association (NBA) took the unusual step of banning the shoes from professional competitions, ruling that they provide 'an undue competitive advantage'. Proving the adage that there is no such thing as bad press, following the NBA ban and the subsequent attention the shoe received, sales began to soar and the original design quickly sold out.

The technology behind the 'Concept 2', referred to by the manufacturers as 'Load 'N Launch', does not create energy for vertical lift but instead amplifies the energy the basketball player is already putting into a pump.

INCYCLE

After research showed that 57 per cent of PUMA's environmental impact is related to the production of raw materials such as leather, cotton and rubber, the company looked at increasing the number of sustainable materials it uses. The resulting InCycle collection is entirely biodegradable or recyclable and 100 per cent 'cradle-to-cradle' certified.

Cradle-to-cradle is a design approach modelled on nature's process of restoring organisms to their constituent nutrients, to be returned to the ecosystem after their natural life cycle. Cradle-to-cradle products can be viewed in the same way. They are designed to be broken down into elements consisting of a single material that is either a technical or a biological nutrient. Technical nutrients, such as plastic and metal, can then be returned to the manufacturing system at the same level as they entered it, rather than mixed with other materials and down-cycled. Biological nutrients are organic materials that can be left to decompose in natural environments, providing food for the local ecosystem.

It is not enough to simply implement thorough recycling processes. For an item to function as a cradle-to-cradle product, it must actually be conceived as one. Cradle-to-cradle products require careful design if they are to break down into single-material components. For products to be biodegradable they must be made only of materials comprised of organic fibres without any toxic chemicals.

The upper part of InCycle biodegradable shoes is made of a mix of organic cotton and linen while the sole is composed of a biodegradable plastic. When they have served their natural life these ingredients can be composted and broken down into their natural building blocks.

Puma InCycle sneakers are just part of a whole biodegradable and fully cradle-to-cradle certified collection. Also in the collection are bags and jackets as well as other apparel and accessories.

INDEX

PICTURE CREDITS

CREDITS

An Hachette UK Company
www.hachette.co.uk

First published in
Great Britain in 2015
by Conran Octopus,
a division of Octopus
Publishing Group Ltd, in
conjunction with the
Design Museum.

Octopus Publishing Group Ltd
Carmelite House
50 Victoria Embankment
London EC4Y 0DZ
www.octopusbooks.co.uk
www.octopusbooksusa.com

Copyright © Octopus
Publishing Group 2015

Distributed in the US by
Hachette Book Group
1290 Avenue of the
Americas, 4th and 5th Floors,
New York, NY 10020

Distributed in Canada by
Canadian Manda Group
664 Annette St., Toronto,
Ontario, Canada M6S 2C8

Alex Newson asserts the
moral right to be identified as
the author of this work.

A CIP catalogue record
for this book is available
from the British Library.

Text written by:
Alex Newson

Commissioning Editor:
Joe Cottington
Consultant Editor:
Deyan Sudjic
Editor:
Pauline Bache
Copy Editor:
Robert Anderson
Design:
Untitled
Picture Researcher:
Sophie Hartley
*Assistant Production
Manager:*
Caroline Alberti

Printed and bound in China
ISBN 978 1 84091 678 2

10 9 8 7 6 5 4 3 2 1